The Young Marine and the Snow

an allegory

Richard W. Linford

The Young Marine and the Snow

an allegory

© Copyright 2009

All rights reserved.

Linford Corporation.

A Sweetwater Book Company publication

First edition

ISBN 1-57574-019-2

Imprint Linford Corporation

[The two cover images were taken from the Internet. There is no indication they are copyrighted. In their form as part of the cover design and as found within this book they are copyrighted © 2009 Linford Corporation All rights reserved.]

AN ALLEGORY

DEDICATED TO

THE UNITED STATES MARINES

AND TO MY FAMILY

The Young Marine and the Snow

Thomas leaned closer. "Take a jacket, hat, gloves, scarf, dark glasses, and long johns if you can lay your hands on a pair at this late hour. Otherwise leave on your pajamas under your pants. Heavy socks and boots. No gym shoes and your sweatshirt with the hood. I bring the food and drink. I've got binoculars.

"I have to teach Sunday school," Andrew hedged. "My lesson is Joseph in Egypt running away from Potipher's wife when she came on to him. Besides I don't have a gun.

Andrew Chipman did not want to go with Thomas to the Book Cliff Mountains. It was too far from Salt Lake City and too much effort. Andrew was decompressing from jet lag from his flight from the Middle East and he did have to teach Sunday school. He worried he might not get back in time.

"Not to worry," Thomas countered. "I'll have you back late Saturday night so you can teach your lesson. My mom read me that Bible story when I was a little boy. Didn't do any good. This trip is my gift to you for serving in Iraq. And you don't need to bring a gun. You carried enough guns in Iraq. I carry a .357 Magnum Colt King Cobra handgun and a Savage rifle shotgun combo with scope that cost me five hundred and fifty four dollars.

"Five hundred dollars?" said Andrew.

"Five hundred and fifty four dollars," Thomas said. "Worth every dollar. Savage was born in Jamaica, lived in Australia, and invented the recoilless rifle. Moved to New York in the late 1800s where he designed the lever action repeating rifle known as the Savage 1889 and later the 99. Started the Savage Arms Company. My .357 is one of the most revered revolvers of all time.

Thomas continued."Same with the cartridge. The Magnum is probably the most popular bullet of all time. The cartridge produces the right amount of recoil an average hunter can control. The .357 is also for killing deer. But you have to use it close up and place your shot. The .357 used to be advertised as the power cartridge. Now the .44 Magnum cartridge and several others are much more powerful than the .357. I use a soft point 158 grain bullet when I hunt mountain lions.

"I thought you were doing your residency in pathology?" said Andrew. "Forget about practicing medicine. You missed your calling. You should be an outfitter. A guide to the Wyoming Tetons. A guide to Idaho and Wyoming and Montana fly fishing. A guide to the Utah Book Cliffs for hunting. Thomas the all around outdoors man. Maybe an extreme safari guy to Botswana or the Tanzania Serengeti.

"Forensic Pathologist!" said Thomas. "I like the detail and the intrigue. My work funds my outdoor hobbies. And you want to be a lawyer? How well are lawyers liked? All those lawyer jokes. If you argue criminal cases, you can put me on the stand as special witness and I will give you my expert scientific opinion. TV shows like CSI and CSI-Miami and CSI-New York make forensics seem easy. But forensic pathology work is much more complex and difficult than is shown on TV.

Thomas needed a breath between pontifications.

"In the nineties a postal worker was charged with murdering a waitress. Based on bite mark evidence presented by one forensic scientist, the postal worker was found guilty and sentenced to death. Last week DNA on saliva found at the crime scene was used by a forensic pathologist to exonerate the postal worker and convict the real killer.

"Andrew, you haven't ridden yet in my new Aspen Metalic Green Ford F 150 truck. I bought the super crew cab. It has the moon roof, BOSE stereo audio, DVD, reverse sensing, four by four drive, eight foot box, and I fitted it with a luxury camper. I even bought the Sirius Satellite Radio package. I saw my Ford F 150 on one of those TV Superbowl ads and again on "24" that TV show with Kiefer Sutherland as Jack Bauer. I started doing some research on the Internet about trucks and before you or Jeb could spell forensic pathologist I am the proud new owner.

"I'll pick you up at 3:30 am. Maria is coming and so is Jeb.

*****

The Ford F 150 tires slapped the icy asphalt.
The heater droned hot on half defrost with half heat to the floor.

Beyond the freeway they inched along a narrow snow-covered lane bordered with high black bushes and trees.
Flickering yard lights framed the dark ranch house, corrals, barn, and sheds against the snow.

Pickups with camper shells, tractors, ATVs, snowmobiles, RVs and camp trailers were silhouetted in moonlight as were dark shadowed horses. Standing in the cold were thirty or so black Angus cattle.

Chained cat hounds barked to crescendo as the Ford F 150 invaded their territory.

You could smell and taste Maria's fresh scent on the hot heater air.

She was curled up asleep in the front seat.

Jeb was much larger than his brother but carbon copy of Thomas's temperament. Jeb drooled as he slept and mumbled fitfully, his head against cold glass of a back door window.

With Jeb, all you have to do is whisper any of the words "food" or "hunt" or "shooting" or "guns" to make Jeb a willing participant.

Thomas gave Jeb the nickname "Shooter" for good reason.

*****

"Bearskin Outfitters has guided hunting parties to the Book Cliffs for fifty years," said Thomas. "The company hunts the Book Cliff area on the eastern side of Utah south of Vernal near the Colorado border. Cougar population has exploded given the increase in the mule deer and elk populations. Bearskin takes groups of hunters in camper trucks and RVs to an area. They set up camp. They drive snowmobiles for miles searching for tracks. Bearskin has brought to bay more Boone and Crocket big game trophy cats than you can count.

Thomas droned.

"A multi-day cougar hunt costs thirty five hundred to five thousand dollars per person. The license costs two hundred and fifty eight dollars. For an extra thousand dollars Bearskin Outfitters will guarantee in writing that you will take home a trophy tom cougar or they will give you your money back. Their prices are skyrocketing because of so much demand. I'll bet they will charge ten thousand dollars per hunt next year. Each season they run hundreds of hunters through their hunting camps.

"Multiply at least one thousand hunters per year times thirty five hundred to five thousand dollars and you've got a business that generates more than three point five to five million dollars in annual revenues. Think about how much money that is when their price is ten thousand dollars per hunt.

"I went on one of their short hunts last year and I thought you might like to see several of their live cougars up close and personal before we drive to the Book Cliffs. Regardless of how experienced you are, there is nothing as visceral as coming face to face with a loose snarling mountain lion. Not even Iraq.

"We probably won't see cougars during our trip but if you go on a Bearskin Outfitters trip, like I said, they guarantee they will deliver you a loose snarling lion which will conjure up one hair raising set of memories. Enough fear to give you nightmares for moons to come.

Thomas and Andrew and Jeb got out of the truck. They stood by long narrow five foot high heavy gauge welded wire cages. In each of six cages, a huge dark snarling cougar paced back and forth in the dark.

"The scary part is not the pacing back and forth," said Thomas. What drives a stake of fear deep in your heart are the eyes. Cougar eyes reflect light turning them into mini-search lights. Mesmerizing. Enough to freeze you solid like Lot's wife into a pillar of salt. Not able to run. Those two moving fire coals in each cage create immense fear. And this is true if you look at them for one minute or stand still and watch them for a long time. Cougar eyes are fearsome, mysterious, bright, hot embers that transfix, rivet, and hypnotize you into jelly or a piece of granite.

Peter, the major owner and massive nearly seven foot tall lead Bearskin guide, came out of the ranch house.

His voice was quiet. It was authoritative. Peter was never out of command. Peter was obeyed at all times by everyone, no exception, no questions asked. Peter's powerful personal influence generated from his size and his Special Forces training. Even Thomas, who was never subservient and seldom if ever stopped talking, closed his mouth and bowed low and scraped to pay Peter deference. Andrew had served in Iraq under unconquerable sergeants like Peter.

When Peter became instructor nobody interrupted.

"We camp at the hunt area in comfortable heated camp trailers." Peter whispered.

"We spend most of our time hunting with the least amount of road time to and from town.

"Go with me on a hunt and you don't go into town to the restaurants, bars, and stores.

"Go with me and you go to hunt on my terms and only on my terms.

"We canvass great concentric circles on snowmobiles

"We drive the mountain roads in four by four trucks or four wheeled ATVs.

"We find fresh cougar tracks, walkie talkie everyone to a rendevous, and turn the dogs loose on the scent and the serious hunt is on.

"The dogs run miles of country following the lion, so we drive in a vehicle as close behind as we can get until we know for sure the dogs have the cat at bay in the rocks or up a tree.

"Each of our dogs wears a remote sensing tracking collar attached to a radio transmitter that transmits a radio telemetry signal on a specified frequency.

"With our receiver we pinpoint the dog's direction and range. We can even tell the dog's behavior.

"Our receivers are sophisticated. They have lights, sound, and a bar graph with LCD screen and a needle indicator.

"Our receivers pick up motion that tells us if a dog is running or standing.

"Our receivers include a bark indicator that tells us if the dog is baying or silent.

"Our receivers tell us if a hound has treed the cougar.

"We operate on five different bands and multiple frequencies within each band so we prevent signal overlap.

"That way we can use multiple collars.

"If a band is numbered 220 and a three digit frequency is 216 then that collar is Band 220 and frequency 216.

"I spent megabucks on my tracking systems.

"The small Salt Lake City company that sells us our tracking collars and receivers also builds and sells expensive tiny falcon tracking systems to falconers including sheiks in Saudi Arabia.

Like the old actor Jack Palance who played Curly in City Slickers, Peter continued his raspy voice whisper.

"Once we know the dogs have cornered the cougar, we hike through the snow.

"We walk at a comfortable pace. No use giving one of my hunters a heart attack.

"The cats weigh in at eighty to one hundred and eighty pounds. A tom averages one hundred and thirty to one hundred and eighty pounds.

"We get you your cougar license over the counter so you don't need to wait to draw a permit.

"At the time you pick up your permit you can add Bobcat, Elk, or Mule Deer depending on the state.

"Each hunt includes lodging and meals in my luxury campers.

"Each hunt includes my guiding, skinning, field butchering, and trophy care.

"I provide taxidermy for added money.

"A sculptor friend of mine Stanley Watts of Atlas Bronze Casting will sculpt and cast your trophy animal in bronze -- for a serious seventy five thousand dollar chunk of change of course.

"Any questions?

*****

Peter had been through his pitch many times selling rich East and West Coast and Texas and German and Japanese Nimrod wannabes.

"Peter sells his hunts to German and Japanese hunters who will pay as much as $50,000 per hunt because of the many added services they demand," Thomas whispered to Andrew.

"Too early in the morning for questions," Andrew said.

Andrew was glad to be back from Iraq. Andrew was not happy about this spur of the moment winter snow safari to the Book Cliff Mountains.

"In fact, I do have one question." Andrew said. "What kind of dogs do you use?"

Pleased with the question, Peter did not break whisper and became the staccato instructor again.

"I've got three powerful solid red pedigreed cat tracking Redbone Coonhounds.

"They are aggressive hunters in mountain, desert or swamp.

"Terrain doesn't matter.

"They are easy to deal with around the house.

"I've got six pedigreed Plott Hounds.

"Forefathers of the Plott Hounds were once used for boar hunting in Germany.

"Jonathon Plott brought some of these boar hounds to North Carolina.

"Through the years there was little cross breeding.

"In 1946, the Plott Hound was registered with the United Kennel Club.

"My Plott dogs have more courage, endurance, strength, and vicious fight than any dog I have found.

"And they are amazingly intelligent.

"And they have a beautiful throat.

"My Redbone Coonhounds are A.K.C. They are surefooted and fast. They can handle any terrain. They have the best cold nose of any hound I've come across.

"Well, enough of this!" Peter raised his voice to full volume.

*****

Peter stepped in disconcertingly close and bent over, peering down on Thomas's diminutive five feet eight inch body, staring Thomas in the eyes.

"You be careful, Thomas.

"Bring your party back alive and unhurt.

"The snow is unforgiving.

"Snow survival is not easy.

"As you know, before I let any hunter travel in snow country, I run him through a five day snow survival basic training and certification course.

"My course includes safety and survival skills and techniques.

"I give specialized equipment training including pickup, four wheeler, snow cat and snowmobile repair.

"I train for ice driving, trailer use, and snowmobile operations under emergency conditions.

"I train predator and other game tracking and analysis.

"My hunters receive gun safety and use and marksmanship training.

"And I provide special emergency survival kits.

"When you buy my hunt you buy my survival skills training course.

"Best in the world.

"Nobody goes on my hunts without my training.

"Nobody!

"I bring all of my hunters back alive.

"Out of thousands of hunters, I haven't lost one.

Peter was on a roll.

"You drive away from the soft security of Salt Lake City.

"You drive yourself out into the snow.

"Before you know it you're in fifty degrees below wind chill or an avalanche or a snow pit or a water hazard or an equipment accident, or animal an attack.

"Each of my managers takes advanced training at my survival academy.

"Each hunter on any hunt of mine gets a two hundred and fifty dollar personal survival kit including a special North Face self-heating jacket, an inflatable vest, and a sub-zero tent.

"Each of my hunters is taught snow cave construction.

"Each hunter knows about avalanches, snow pits, water hazards and how to cope.

"A snow avalanche can move at speeds of eighty to a hundred miles per hour, suck up and bury a snowmobile or hunter or set of dogs in seconds.

"Like I monitor my dogs, I give each person use of a five hundred dollar electronic beacon and transceiver, a digital transceiver system with dual antennas and microprocessors that can triangulate a buried person's position.

"If one of my hunters gets hit with an avalanche or falls in a snow pit or falls through the ice in a water hazard, I have a way to find him or her immediately and possibly save a life.

"I give each of my hunters a multifunction outdoor watch that tells time, altitude and barometric pressure and comes with a built-in compass.

"I give each of my hunters topographical maps and I provide training in reading the maps.

"I train them in survival search and rescue day or night, snow or sleet, harsh or easy weather.

"And once more, my hunters come for the hunt.

"They don't go to town for any reason.

"Peter loves to hear himself talk. But then Peter is passionate about what he does. Besides, anyone nearly seven feet tall with Special Forces training can talk all he wants and for as long as he wants. The bear sleeps any place he wants to," thought Andrew. "Anyway," Andrew muttered, " Peter spoke the survival truth.

"Sounds like the marines," Andrew said. "Come back alive. Come back unhurt. Come back a survivor. Just like my Marine Sergeant," Andrew complimented Peter.

The stop took sixty five minutes and they were on the road again.

*****

Driving past Park City.

They stopped at Kamas at a small crowded diner.

A number of locals.

Several truck drivers.

One tall red mane driver wore a see through tank top and cut off shorts.

"Crazy as a loon to dress like that in dead of Utah winter," said Jeb out loud within earshot of the truck drivers.

While the waitress brought the eggs, hash browns, bacon, sausage, pancakes, orange juice, syrup, and hot cocoa, the red mane driver leered at Maria.

Nursing last night's beer or hard liquor hangover, he stood behind her and put his hands on her shoulders.

Without looking up from his breakfast, Andrew said quietly. "Take your hands off the lady."

With unfounded bravado the truck driver stared into Andrews' eyes.

He left his hands where they were and started moving them downward saying, "But I don't see no lady."

Andrew came up out of his chair in a smooth arc.

Before the red mane driver could move his hands half an inch, Andrew had smashed him in the side of the head with his boot.

The red mane driver dropped out cold in the aisle without a grunt not knowing he had just been kicked by a ranked kick boxer and seasoned marine,

Andrew's martial arts display was ill timed. At that same moment, the Summit County Sheriff and her deputy came through the door of the diner. They were holding coffee mugs.

Having half witnessed Andrew's battery on the fallen truck driver, they dropped their mugs, drew their pistols, and confronted Andrew who in a low, patient voice explained what had just happened.

After listening to witnesses, including Betsy, the owner of the diner, they water doused and handcuffed the truck driver, got their coffee, and took him outside to their police car.

*****

There was short lived deference by Thomas.

Jeb's respect was long lived. Jeb opened the door of the truck for Andrew.

Maria was all admiration.

Maria made no effort to hide her effort to draw Andrew into serious conversation.

Her attempts irritated Thomas, this forensic pathologist doctor, who considered Maria to be his prized, highly intellectual, beautiful, trophy woman.

"How long were you in Iraq?" Maria asked.
"Too long, was Andrew's quiet answer.

"Going back to school?

"Yes.

"Where?

"University of Utah for an MBA and law degree.

"Your mom and dad still alive?

"Yes.

"Brothers and sisters?

"Two brothers and a sister. One brother still in Iraq.

"How hard is it to be a Marine?

"Hardest thing a man can do.

"You married?

"No.

"Girl friend?

"No.

Maria processed Andrew's comments.

"What characterizes one of your few, proud, brave marines?" Maria asked.

"By My Rifle, the creed of a United States Marine, by Major General WH Rupertus," said Andrew.

"Do you know your creed by heart?" asked Maria.

"Yes, ma'am."

"Repeat it for me," Maria said.

"This is my rifle," intoned Andrew.

"There are many like it, but this one is mine.

"My rifle is my best friend. It is my life.

"I must master it as I must master my life.

"My rifle without me is useless. Without my rifle, I am useless.

"I must fire my rifle true.

"I must shoot straighter than my enemy who is trying to kill me.

"I must shoot him before he shoots me. I will…

"My rifle and myself know that what counts in war is not the rounds we fire,

"The noise of our bursts, nor the smoke we make.

"My rifle is human, even as I, because it is my life.

"Thus, I will learn it as a brother.

"I will learn its weaknesses, its strengths, its parts, its accessories, its sights, and its barrel.

"I will ever guard it against the ravages of weather and damage.
"I will keep my rifle clean and ready, even as I am clean and ready.

"We will become part of each other. We will …

"Before God I swear this creed.

"My rifle and myself are the defenders of my country.

"We are the masters of our enemy.

"We are the saviors of my life.

"So be it, until there is no enemy, but peace."

Maria clapped.

Jeb clapped.

Thomas turned on his new Sirius satellite radio.

Andrew thought about what Peter said about not letting his hunters go into town.

*****

To avoid Maria's wanton stare, Andrew bent his head and read.

Driving southeast from Vernal toward and into the Book Cliff Mountains, the snow got deeper by the quarter hour.

The country road was marked by tops of fence lines.

Once in a while there was evidence a grader or snow plow had been along.

The sun was up.

The glare was intense.

Thanks for sun glasses.

Andrew paid little attention to where they were or where they were going.

After the first five minutes it all looked the same.

Mile after mile after mile of low hill snowfields.

Snow undulating like sea waves far into the distance lapping up against the higher Book Cliff Mountains.

A periodic farm yard.

Now and then a ranch house.

No cattle or horses in any field.

It was bitter cold outside.

"Like Peter said, wind chill out there could well be fifty below," thought Andrew.

Above the blaring country music, and to cut through the boredom and monotony of the trip, Andrew started reading out loud the travel brochures and flyers he picked up at the gas station in Vernal, top noting trivia factoids.

"Vernal is green and tree shaded.

"Surrounding Vernal is dry farming and ranching country.

"Vernal is a jumping off point for Dinosaur National Monument, Flaming Gorge National Recreation Area, and the Uinta Mountains.

"Vernal has a few motels, cafes, and fast food restaurants.

"Vernal has a good prehistory museum, several movie theaters and water slides for the kids.

"Vernal is located along Highways 191 and 40 in the northeast corner of Utah southeast of the Uinta Mountains, 35 miles south of Flaming Gorge and 20 miles west of Dinosaur National Monument.

"At the entrance to its Main Street is a huge pink dinosaur holding a sign which says Vernal Utah's Dinosaur Land.

"Population in 2004 was 7,939 with 3,786 males and 3,928 females.

"Elevation is 5,322 feet.

"Vernal is in Uintah County, Utah.

"Land area is 4.6 square miles.

"Zip code: 84078.

"Median resident age 28.3.

"Median household income $30,357 in 2000.

"Median house value $81,000 in the year 2000.

"White Non-Hispanic population is 91.8%.

"Hispanic 4.4%.

"American Indian 3.1%.

"Two or more races 1.4%.

"Other race 1.2%.

"Ancestries are English 26%, German 12.3%, U.S. 8.3%, Irish 8%, Danish 4.6%, Norwegian 4.1%.

"For population 25 years and over 81.9% complete high school or higher. Bachelor's degree 14.6%; Graduate or professional: 3.1%. Unemployment 6.3%;

"Mean travel time to drive to work in Vernal is 16 minutes.

"For the population 15 years and over 22.9% never married. 57.5% are now married. 2.6% are separated. 5.5% are widowed. 11.5% divorced. 1.6% foreign born.

"Population change in 1990 was a positive 1,067, a 16.1% increase."

Jeb tuned out trying to sleep.

Thomas tuned out trying his cell phone over and over again.

Maria listened to Andrew's mind numbing detail.

*****

Maria reached back and took the booklet out of Andrew's hands.

She read out loud.

"On a map of the west you plot Vernal slightly southeast of Salt Lake City, slightly north west of Denver, almost south of Billings Montana, north west of Albuquerque.

"Las Vegas is to the southwest.

"One finds in the Vernal area white water rafting, hunting and fishing, cross country skiing, hiking in remote mountain ranges, snowmobiling, and boating.

"The town has several small movie theaters.

"Vernal was rated the 48th best small town in America and is known for its traditional family and community values.

"It is known for the faith, hard work and patriotism of its citizens.

"The Dinosaur National Monument and Quarry is visited by people from all over the world.

"Vernal has a Museum and Dinosaur Gardens.

"It boasts the PRCA Dinosaur Round-Up Rodeo.

"It has wild horses, oil wells, killer mean thunderstorms, with gorgeous sunrises.

"The Vernal Field Office for the BLM manages 1.8 million surface acres and 2.5 million sub-surface acres of public lands together with 1.3 million acres of National Forest System lands for which it regulates mineral development.

"It has Native American trust responsibilities for mineral development tied to Tribal and allotted Indian mineral leases.

"It gives oversight to oil and gas development, recreation, wildlife, cultural resources, lands, rangeland management, riparian rights, fire management, forestry, wild horses, law enforcement resource protection, and wilderness."

"Vernal is home to the fifty first Mormon temple.

"To the northeast of Vernal, just outside of Measer, Utah, and in a canyon, is a giant American Flag painted sixty to one hundred feet up on a sheer rock cliff face together with a painting of the motto "Remember the Maine." The sinking of the Maine started the Spanish-American war.

"Vernal is Uintah County's largest city; is located in eastern Utah near the Colorado State Line; is 175 miles east of Salt Lake City. It is bordered on the north by the Uinta Mountains, one of the few mountains ranges in the world which lie in an east-west rather than usual north to south direction.

"The Book Cliff Mountains lie to the south, Blue Mountains to the east, while Vernal lies in the Ashley Valley, named for William H. Ashley, an early fur trader who came to the Vernal area in 1825.

At which point and to Thomas' growing consternation, Jeb came alive to this game of reading out loud.

*****

Jeb took the book from Maria and read.

"Vernal, unlike the majority of Utah towns, was not settled initially by Mormon pioneers.

"Brigham Young sent a scouting party to the Uinta Basin in 186.

"The scouting party reported back that the area was good for nothing but nomad purposes, hunting grounds for Indians and "to hold the world together."

"That same year, President Abraham Lincoln set the area aside as the Uintah Indian Reservation and named Captain Pardon Dodds Indian agent for this new reservation."

"When Dodds retired, he moved to Ashley Valley to raise livestock, along with agency workers, Morris Evans and John Blankenship.

"They arrived on 14 February 1873 and settled on Ashley Creek and Dodds built the first cabin in the valley, located about four miles northwest of present day Vernal.

"Many single men--trappers, prospectors, home seekers, and drifters--arrived in Ashley Valley, and some stayed.

"There wasn't a woman in the area until 1876.

"Remember that fact," said, Maria. "Not one woman in the area until 1876."

Jeb continued.

"The area where Vernal is now located was called the Bench, and it was described as a large barren cactus flat.

"The David Johnston family moved onto the Bench on 6 June 1878.

" David took his shovel from the wagon and cleared off the cactus so his children could stand without getting cactus needles in their feet.

"David put the wagon on logs to keep it off the ground as there were so many lizards, horned toads, scorpions, mice, and rattlesnakes.

"Alva Hatch came to the valley looking for a place to locate in May 1878.

"He returned later with his family and his father, Jeremiah Hatch, along with Jeremiah's two wives.

"The fall of 1879 brought many settlers to the valley.

*****

"Two wives, huh." Maria snorted. Maria took the book back and read.

"On 29 September 1879 the Meeker Massacre occurred in Colorado.

"White River Utes killed their agent, Nathan Meeker, among others.

"Renegade Utes rode to Ashley Valley to convince the Uintah Utes to join them in killing all the white people in the area.

"Instead, the Uintah chiefs advised the settlers to "fort-up.

"A fort was built on the Bench due to its open expanse.

"Settlers of Ashley Valley took their cabins apart, moving them to the fort site.

"The incident with the Indians was settled, but the people remained in the fort that winter.

"The winter was severe, killing most of the animals.

"The settlers suffered.

"Much of their grain had been gathered from the ground, since grasshoppers had knocked it from the plant stocks.

"The grain became moldy.

"Diphtheria took its toll.

"It was March before they could get out of the valley for supplies."

"Fancy that, said Maria," tossing the book to Andrew who continued reading out loud.

*****

"Families moved their cabins back to their homesteads, while others remained in the fort.

"A town grew out of the fort and became known as Ashley Center.

"A store was opened and the residents applied for a post office.

"The name Ashley Center was requested, but it was too similar to the town of Ashley; therefore, the name Vernal was assigned to the community by the U.S. Postal Department.

"The settlers developed an irrigation system that serves the valley today.

"Because of the distance to a major railhead, settlers produced, manufactured, and developed most everything they needed.

"The leading livelihood was cattle and sheep.

"Milling, the production of honey, and the farming of grains and alfalfa were also important.

"Vernal still is without a railroad.

"The highway transportation system helps residents access most good and services.

"Although The Church of Jesus Christ of Latter-day Saints, the Mormons, helped to set up Vernal as a town in 1884, the town wasn't incorporated until 1897.

"Vernal had the distinction of being a city without taxation for fifteen years.

"In 1948 Vernal had its first oil boom.

"From that time it has been a boom and bust town.

"The thriving tourist business to Dinosaur National Monument, plus livestock and agriculture production, keep Vernal going during "bust" times.

"Flaming Gorge Dam was built in 1964, bringing more tourists to the area. Steinaker and Red Fleet dams, built in 1962 and 1980, provide irrigation water and recreation.

"Big stores moved to the outskirts of town, but small businesses keep the downtown area alive.

"Vernal is county seat and draws from a county population of 22,211 and from western Colorado.

*****

"Knock it off! Knock it off! Knock it off! Knock off the reading!" Thomas shouted and turned up the radio music volume to the max.

Thomas was red, agitated, angry, suffering some weird, wild, apoplectic, livid fit.

Big Jeb grabbed the book from Andrew.

Jeb raised his voice to a shout and read on and this now tedious game which was first conceived to break the trip monotony and which had evolved as a way to suffocate Thomas' egotistical chatter, turned spitefully and sibling deadly.

"The Book Cliffs is a part of the East Tavaputs Plateau that begins near Green River, Utah and extends eastward into Colorado," yelled Jeb over the blare of the radio.

"The area begins about 50 air miles south of Vernal, Utah and extends south to the Book Cliffs divide. Towards the east is the Colorado/Utah state line.

"The Uintah and Ouray Indian Reservation is on the west side of the Book Cliffs. Both southern Uintah County and northern Grand County are included.

"This unique Book Cliffs area contains widely diverse landscapes.

"The area begins in the northern desert shrub zone at about 5,500 feet and rises southward to nearly 8,500 feet into the aspen and fir zones.

"The area between consists of broad sagebrush and pinion/juniper vistas broken by deep valleys, some containing perennial streams.

"Approximately 70% of the area is administered by the BLM, 25% by the School and Institutional Trust Land Administration (SITLA), and 5% is private.

"The area is uniquely rich in both renewable and nonrenewable resources.

"Resource values include abundant wildlife, hydrocarbon resources (primarily natural gas, oil shale and tar sands), livestock grazing, a variety of recreational pursuits, and a small timber resource.

"As of the end of 1996, there were 144 oil and gas federal leases.

"Additionally, there were 50 wells on federal and state oil and gas leases that were either actively producing or capable of production.

"Wildlife species in the area include mule deer, Rocky Mountain elk, antelope, mountain lion, black bear, waterfowl, shorebirds, blue and sage grouse, golden eagle, hawks and owls, as well as many small mammals, birds, amphibians and reptiles.

"Moose, bison and Rocky Mountain bighorn sheep are seen.

"Endangered species are bald eagle, ferruginous hawk, and peregrine falcon.

"The Book Cliffs provide habitat for other endangered or sensitive species.

"Colorado River cutthroat trout are native to the area.

"And habitat exists for the Mexican spotted owl.

"The area includes critical summer and winter ranges for wildlife.

"The limiting factor for deer and elk in most ecosystems is lack of winter range.

"Livestock grazing is authorized.

"The area is currently grazed by livestock belonging to local ranchers.

"Recreation opportunities draw so many visitors to the area such that unplanned trails and tracks are causing erosion.

"Opportunities for wildlife viewing and solitude abound.

"The heaviest visitor use occurs during fall hunting seasons; but, other recreational use is increasing.

"Off-road vehicle use causes increased destruction of vegetation, leading to accelerated soil erosion and a myriad of unplanned trails and tracks.

"Ranching is a vital part of the Book Cliffs. Burt and Christine DeLambert own and operate the DeLambert Ranch.

"Alameda Corporation purchased the S & H Ranch and some of the grazing privileges associated with the Cripple Cowboy Ranch.

"BLM Public Information Sheet 1998.

Jeb stopped reading.

Jeb's satisfaction was perverse.

Jeb savored the moment.

For those few minutes he felt total control over his overbearing brother.

The three of them had ganged up on Thomas.

Yet Thomas knew what was going on into the second reading.

Thomas, the borderline genius forensic pathologist, was not slow on the uptake.

Fuming.

Seething,

Thomas suffered this reading mockery for what seemed to him like an eon, not talking, bottling it up, until at last he reached tipping point, lost it, blew his cork, and shouted his vicious outburst.

*****

On the left side of the road, the six point buck deer stood in snow up to its belly.

Immovable.

Somehow thinking standing still created invisibility.

Frightened eyes.
Probably does with fawns nearby.

Thomas slowed the Ford F 150.

Rolled down his window.

The freezing cold turned the pickup interior into a meat locker.

The big buck was transfixed.

Maria, Jeb, and Andrew mesmerized.

Thomas lifted his .357 Magnum Colt King Cobra handgun.

The deafening concussion rocked the world inside and outside the cab of the Ford F 150.

The huge buck took a step.

It crumpled in blood spattered snow.

He did not die.

He lay in snow mixed gore.

Bleating.

Heaving sides.

Large staring eyes.

Looking deep into his tormenter's eyes.

Questioning the executioner.

Thomas fired off the second Magnum round.

He stopped the truck.

He stepped down onto the road.

Brown shapes bounded toward brush and a low tree thicket.

Thomas fired four more rounds at the does and fawns.

"Can't tell if I hit one or not," he shouted.

His serrated skinning knife was out.

He ripped the deer belly.

Disemboweling the hapless buck with swift movements.

His out of season evil poaching took less than five minutes.

"Venison tonight," he shouted.

"Venison tonight," he sang.

With gleeful ceremony, Thomas wrapped the carcass in a plastic sheet.

He imperiously commandeered Jeb to help him lift it onto the roof of the camper and tie it down.

Trophy buck by anyone's standard.

Premeditated revenge on his three reader tormenters.

"Amazing he didn't bolt and run," said Thomas.

"Venison tonight," Thomas hummed his little tune.

"Venison tonight."

Andrew was sick to his stomach.

Maria buried her head in her coat.

Her first time on a kill.

None excepting perhaps Thomas anticipated a bloody Book Cliffs trip.

A diabolical drama.

Maria stepped out of the truck and threw up.

*****

"Forensic pathologist," thought Andrew. "Butcher pathologist.

Andrew tried to pray in his mind but words would not form.

The surrounding sterile snow world was devoid of spiritual meaning.

"The coward," he thought.

"The damnable, modern, biblical Nimrod.

"Poacher.

"Killing that innocent animal for the sake of killing.

"Nimrod is from the Hebrew verb marad meaning "The Rebel against God."

"The Bible describes Nimrod as this mighty hunter before the LORD.

"As this diabolical man with total contempt for God.

"This ruthless man lusting for power.

"This first tyrant.

"This first man who taught other men to kill and eat animals,

"This Satan worshipper.

"This builder of the Babylonian pyramid ziggurat with its fertility rites temple on its peak.

This satanic temple used in worshipping Satan.

"This temple from which Nimrod satisfied his sexual lusts while shooting arrows into heaven in defiance of God.

"The work of building the tower of Babel was interrupted by God who caused the babel of confusing languages to prevent Nimrod from obtaining power and control over all peoples of the earth.

"After their deaths, Nimrod and his wife Semiramis were revered as ancient king and queen of heaven, confirmed as gods, receiving status and homage as Marduk and Astarte.

"Josephus says Nimrod taught men "to esteem it … cowardice to submit to God."

"It is said that Nimrod, having access to a prophesy about Abraham, and as precursor to the later killing of the infants by evil King Herod at time of Christ, sacrificed seventy thousand boy babies trying to prevent Abraham's birth.

"Nimrod built his tower ostensibly as prevention against drowning by another flood.

"In reality, he used that excuse to energize the people to work on the project.

"In fact, he built the tower to exercise Satanic dictatorial, genocidal, infanticidal control over all mankind.

"Some say the tower was built to get to the City of Enoch which was still visible.

"One account states that Nimrod died a violent death, killed by a wild animal -- a fitting death for a butcher.

"Venison tonight," sang Thomas.

"Forget that," whispered Andrew.

"What did you say?" snarled Thomas.

They drove on and on into the snowy still undulating snow ocean of the lower Book Cliffs.

The snowmobile trailer with its four black snowmobile steeds dutifully trailed on behind.

"You disapprove of me, don't you." Thomas whispered to Andrew.

"You disapprove of me, don't you," Thomas whispered to Maria.

"You disapprove of me, don't you," Thomas raised his voice at Jeb.

"You disapprove of the doctor pathologist.

"The doctor, pathological!" said Andrew.

No one spoke for a longest time.

"Poaching is such a rush." Thomas said, "dissing" and disregarding Andrew's "pathological" comment.

Andrew said again. "Cold blooded.

"You mean cold blooded murder, don't you?" Thomas whispered.

Thomas was smiling.

His eyes were vicious and malevolent.

"Not much different from what you marines did in Iraq," said Thomas.

"I've read the accounts.

"I've watched the videos of your cowardly exploits.

"Not much different today from what you did in Iraq yesterday at Tikrit, is it, Andrew?

"Butchering civilian mothers and dads and teenagers and little children.

"Not so," said Andrew. We had just cause and license and we were fired upon.

*****

It was then Andrew certified the immense hatred Thomas had for him.

Andrew had always felt uncomfortable around Thomas.

Now Andrew knew.

That was why Thomas was so insistent.

That was why Thomas invited him.

To Lord it over him.

Even to do him in.

The trip was manifestation of the arch ethical power struggle between the two of them.

The new Ford F 150.

The expensive guns.

The stop at the Outfitter ranch.

The lavish breakfast at the Kamas café paid for by Thomas.

The newest best snowmobiles.

The doctor title used by Thomas so frequently during the trip.

Andrew had grown up with Thomas.

They were neighbors.

Andrew went to high school and college with Thomas.

They were roommates for a time.

Andrew knew now he had walked in stupor if not stupid.

How could he have missed Thomas's bitter envy all those years.

Andrew, the athlete, scholar, dedicated Church deacon, teacher, and priest.

Andrew, the focused LDS missionary to Holland and Belgium.

Andrew, the warrior marine.

Thomas, the forensic pathological pathologist.

Thomas, the spiritually anemic, physical weakling.

Thomas, the "wannabe popular" who couldn't cut it.

Andrew serving his country in Iraq,

Thomas completing medical school and on his way to being filthy rich.

Andrew putting his life on the line in Iraq firefights,

Thomas hunting cougars with hounds in the Book Cliff Mountains.

Andrew said no more in response to Thomas's taunts about Iraq.

What was there to say, anyway?

*****

They drove on and on and on in silence, ever more engulfed by the expansive never ending low rolling ocean waves of snow.

Thomas driving on and on.

To the top of one hill of white snow.

Coasting to the bottom.

Up.

Down.

Rolling.

Riding.

Sailing.

On and through the glaring, low, roller coaster waves – the sea of never ending white snow.

Thomas driving them beyond the gas tank point of return.

Four red drops of deer blood spattering on the side window.

One drop of sacred blood for each of them, thought Andrew.

The plastic drop cloth had worked loose.

On one side of the truck were thousands of crisscrossing snowmobile tracks.

Snowmobile graffiti running up and down and over small mountains or large mogul-like mounds.

On the other side of the truck were no snowmobile tracks at all.

Only the longest flat expanse of lake snow far as eye could see.

One lone barren tree standing in the middle of this immense lake of snow –

One single, silent, thermometer sentinel monitoring the double digit wind chill while standing guard against intruders.

"Stop the truck! Stop the truck!" Jeb's nose pressed against the window.

Thomas stopped the pickup and Jeb got out, skip hopping on the road back and forth.

"Fresh cougar tracks. Big cougar tracks." Jeb yelped. "Heading out across the frozen lake. Crank up the snowmobiles!

Not stopping to wonder why a big cat was crossing on the lake of snow, they unloaded the snowmobiles readying them for the race.

All the time Thomas boasted to Andrew how he splurged on his four snowmobiles.

"I bought the black with yellow trim YAMAHA APEX RTX, Genesis 150 FI, four-stroke powered, boldly styled, rough-trail ready snowmobile with manufacturer's sticker retail price of ten thousand five hundred and ninety nine dollars each." Thomas rehearsed the ad copy he had memorized.

"Multiply that out and add tax and I paid more than forty five thousand dollars just for the snowmobiles not including the enclosed trailer, snowmobile suits, helmets, gloves and luxury accessories.

Maria threw a black jump suit and a colored helmet at Andrew.

In ten minutes they had the snowmobiles unloaded, mounted, and fired up.

On their sleek, black metal race horses they roared off, following the huge cougar tracks.

Black visors down, casting great plumes of snow, they raced through the white powder toward the sun.

What first looked in the distance to be a small black or tan house cat galloped away from them.

Thomas whooped and he hollered.

Thomas raced way out front with Savage rifle shotgun with scope strapped to his back like a cross country Olympic biathlon skier rifle shooter banshee.

Jeb with a like but garbled incoherent war cry rode behind Thomas brandishing Thomas' .357 Magnum.

Andrew followed far behind, tentative, hesitating, slowing, at greater and greater distance behind Jeb and Thomas.

Maria slowed well behind Andrew.

*****

The separate sounds of the four snowmobiles combined in a weird quartet of cacophony, this screeching harmony that heralded something terrible.

Four black horsemen of the apocalypse.

Four black horsemen rendezvousing with death.

"Four evil black knights on horseback," thought Andrew. Two of them screeching and screaming like banshees across the blinding snow.

Thomas and Jeb were upon the huge tom cougar.

Circling it.

Chasing it.

Herding it with their horses.

Their engines achieving higher and higher and higher pitch.

Deafening.

The great cougar snarled in defiance.

The great cougar ran zig zag toward the lone gray sentinel witness tree.

Barren except for the lone cross bar branch fifteen feet above the snow.

Thomas chasing forward.

Jeb following hard behind.

Thomas at full throttle.

Jeb at full throttle.

Andrew third but both he and Maria much farther behind.

All four snowmobiles flying over the frozen snow lake.

Thirty

Forty.

Fifty miles per hour.

The huge tom cougar ran like Hades.

Ghost-like against the snow.

Running like one of the six Olympians.

Streaking like one of the six children of Kronos and Rhea.

Naked for all the world to see.

Racing like Hades Lord of the Underworld who chose HELL as his own private subterranean kingdom and dominion.

Reaching the barren tree.

Climbing the barren tree in massive bounds.

Achieving the cross bar.

Clinging to the cross bar.

Hiding behind the cross bar.

Thomas stopping his fearful steed.

Thomas firing his Savage at the cougar.

Hitting the tree.

Hitting the cross bar.

Missing the cougar.

Then Thomas was gone.

In an instant, pathological pathologist Thomas was gone.

His black horse was gone.

His Savage rifle was gone.

Leaving not a trace.

Disappearing.

Completely.

Inexorably.

Inevitably.

Forever.

No Tracker DTS.

No dual antennas.

No microprocessors.

No triangulation to buried Thomas's icy watery position.

No air, ground, water search or rescue.

Down.

Down in an instant.

Diving to some extreme depth of darkness.

Lost.

Frozen forever in black water hell.

It is said when mortals kneel before cold hearted Hades, he metes out somber judgment and justice.

It is said none escape his grasp and leave the frozen ice or fiery reach of his clutches.

Thomas, swallowed alive in a white black blinding flash.

Eaten alive by the snow ocean black lake leviathan.

Gone without a trace.

Thomas solo diving to his icy death.

Taking his black horse with him.

*****

Jeb slowed to stop where he had last seen Thomas.

Andrew slowed to a stop far behind Jeb.

Nausea salted Andrew's recurring extreme combat fear,

There was not even a stretch of black water.

Snow covered everything.

Maria stopped her black steed close to Andrew.

Without the high pitched noise of the snowmobiles, the quiet on the vast snow lake was deafening.

*****

In defiance the cougar screamed at the three of them.

Screamed again.

Screamed again.

Screamed again.

Was it possible the great cougar knew what he was doing?

Had he lured them onto the ice?

Could it be?

Was this catamount animal capable of carrying out a diabolical plan.

Big Shooter Jeb wept, pawing at his eyes.

Big Shooter Jeb screamed back at the cougar.

And the great cougar screamed back at Big Shooter Jeb.

Jeb fired Thomas's Magnum at the cougar.

Over and over and over and over and over.

Missing shot after shot just like Thomas the great marksman missed every shot with his Savage rifle shotgun.

Hitting the bar cross.

Missing the cougar.

Emptying the pistol.

*****

Motioning to Maria, Andrew started, revved and wheeled his black snowmobile to gallop then race toward the pickup.

Maria moments behind him.

Andrew could feel seismic movement under his weight.

Urgently accelerating.

Above the roar of the machines, Andrew felt, heard, sensed, tasted all at once ice starting to crack all around them.

Sliding onto the edge, Andrew and Maria looked back.

Scanning the snow lake for big Jeb.

The Savage concussions had dropped Thomas into his instant black water grave.

Jeb's Magnum concussions augmented by great cougar screams sent Jeb into that same horrible heart of darkness.

*****

Andrew spoke to Maria in quiet, solemn preacher's sermon voice.

Andrew spoke to himself.

Andrew spoke to all nature.

Andrew spoke to God.

Andrew shook uncontrollably.

Andrew babbled, experiencing those same feelings he felt in Iraq.

Frenetic.

Frenzied.

Transported with fear or rage.

Transported by violent emotions.

Like he felt after the firefight at Tikrit.

Andrew was talking past Maria.

Talking to himself.

Talking to God.

Talking to the universe.

"Twenty insurgents fired on us in ambush of our convoy.

"Ten of our marines were killed.

"They were backed by more than two hundred fighters in nearby farm buildings.

"When it was over we found there were two hundred and twenty to seventy and then sixty marines.

"We had to leave our ten dead.

"We divided our sixty into six small groups.

"My ten sought the enemy at a nearby farmhouse from which multiple machine gun rounds were fired.

Andrew was on emotional overload.

"Frequent, intense combat experiences do that to you," Andrew said.

"Difficulty sleeping.

"Unable to talk about it.

"Thoughts of suicide.

"Conflicting thoughts.

"Highly aggressive martial arts actions.

"Violent thoughts.

"Like the red mane trucker situation at the cafe.

"Fear of death.

"Actual death.

"Unremitting gut wrenching physical and mental stress.

"The cluster bombs.

"Gun fire.

"Hundreds of deaths from our war and daily Iraqi civil war.

"We engaged," said Andrew.

"I must fire my rifle true.

"I must shoot straighter than my enemy who is trying to kill me.

"I must shoot him before he shoots me. I will…

"My rifle and myself know that what counts in war is not the rounds we fire," intoned Andrew.

"We took out the machine gunners.

"We took out everyone in the farm house including civilians.

"Women and children.

"Old men, young men, boys and girls.

"When the fire fight was over, hundreds were dead.

"They were strewn all round the farm house.

"They were in the yard between the farm buildings.

"Bodies everywhere.

"Our teams of ten continued the fire fight for hours into the other farm buildings and homes.

"We called in air support.

"Of our sixty, seven were wounded.

"Of several hundred insurgents, five survived.

"It was not beautiful.

"We won because we knew what we had to do.

"We knew how to do it.

"And we did it.

"We seized five remaining suspects.

"We seized huge quantities of ammunition including small and large weapons with a huge cache of materials for making suicide bombs.

"There was talk of charging the sixty of us with war crimes.

"Bottom line, we were fired upon.

"We did what we had to do."

*****

Maria was sobbing.

Clinging to him.

The doors to the Ford F 150 were locked.

Habit on Thomas's part.

More blood had dripped to freeze on the side window.

The great tom cougar screamed in the near distance.

A second cougar screamed.

A third.

A fourth.
A fifth.

Andrew ran to the snowmobile trailer.

After frantic search, he found a tire iron.

"The rest of the tools must be in the camper," he thought.

He raced to the truck and pried at the window.

Barely avoiding breaking the window, he opened the door.

Andrew herded, lifted and pushed Maria inside.

He leap climbed the side of the camper to pull the plastic wrapped deer off the top.

He dragged it in front of the truck to open the plastic.

He drove their snowmobiles onto the trailer and locked them in place.

He ran back to the truck, clambered fell inside, and locked the doors.

Twenty minutes later, he and Maria were hostage to first one, then two, then three, then four, then five large cougars.

*****

"The great tom, his wife, and children," thought Andrew.

The lions snarled, growled and prowled.

In plain view on the white road in front of the truck, the lions feasted at their luxury plastic dining table

The cougars knew well their hostages in the truck were a second meal.

If only they could find the point of entry.

Two hours passed.

Andrew hotwired the truck to start the motor and heater.

The five catamounts did not flinch from their raw deer meat dinner.

The night was still.

The moon like a giant floodlight bathed everything in white.

Andrew and Maria could hear each raucous detail as the five cougar ate their deer dinner.

Breaking bones.

Ripping flesh.

*****

As diversion, Andrew read out loud from a book about cougars Thomas left in the cab.

"Felis concolor."

"Cat of a single color.

"Ghost walker.

"Ghost cat.

"Ghost of the wilderness.

"Mythical.

"Legendary.

"Mysterious.

"Secretive.

"Whisp of smoke.

"Ethereal.

"Enigmatic.

"Catamount.

"Cougar.

"Puma.

"Mountain lion.

"A large cat yet smaller than an African lion.

"Larger than a Lynx.

"Larger than a Bobcat.

"Five and one half to eight feet long.

"Eighty to one hundred and eighty pounds in weight.

"Buff, cinnamon, tawny to reddish brown to shades of gray.

"White chested and white muzzle including upper lip, chin, and throat.

"Muzzle with a black dark triangular marking on each side.

"Penetrating eyes.

"Long, cylindrical tail.
"Nocturnal.

"Seldom seen.

"Secretive to a fault.

"Staying in rocks, brush or dense trees for stalking purposes.

"Generally solitary.

"Stealthy in winter, spring, summer or fall.

"Cougars kill people.

"Usually the females breed at eighteen to twenty four months and every two to three years thereafter.

"Mating takes place any time.

"Gestation for a litter is 92 days.

"Cubs have blue eyes when born.

"Cubs have a spotted coat for the first two years.

"For the first two years the cubs stay with their mother.

"She teaches them survival skills.

"Cubs eat meat at six weeks but nurse until three months.

"It was unusual to fine five large cougars together like this.

"Cougars eat everything!

"Mice.

"Deer.

"Elk.

"Rabbits.

"Beaver.

"Skunks.

"Porcupines.

"Martens.

"Foxes.

"Coyotes.

"Peccaries.

"Bear cubs.

"Antelope.

"Rocky Mountain goats.

"Grouse.

"Pheasants.

"Wild turkeys.

"Birds of every kind.

"Fish.

"Pigs.
"Chickens.

"Sheep and lambs.

"Cattle and calves.

"Horses and foals.

"Adult humans and their children"

"Young adults," thought Andrew.

"Cougars think nothing of covering as many as 175 square miles hunting for prey.

"They build "scrapes" which are mounds of dirt, urine, dung, and forest litter to mark their territory against the same sex.

"Most defense of territory is by mutual avoidance versus confrontation.

"Cougars have suffered habitat loss but they are not on anyone's endangered or threatened list.

"Cougars are capable of lethal attacks on children and adults.

"The cougar lives virtually anywhere -- in coniferous forests, swamps, tropical forests, grasslands, chaparral,

"They live in Canada, U.S., Mexico, and Central America.

"They are found in brush, desert, or rocky terrain, wherever you find deer.

"Dominant males kill other males, females and kittens.

"Cougars climb trees with ease.

"They run short distances with ease.

"The scream of the cougar was a death warning to Walapais of Arizona and to the Apaches.

"Indian mythology considers the cougar to be the great symbol of cunning, strength, and ability.

"Indians consider the cougar as mighty hunter.

"Peruvians worshipped the puma as symbol of bravery.

"Dried paws and claws of cougars were used by medicine men to ward off diseases and evil spirits.

"After death of her baby, Cheyenne legend tells of a Native American woman pressing an orphan cougar kitten against her breast until it suckled.

"The woman raised the kitten until in time it would hunt and bring meat to the woman and share.

"The story is that other Cheyenne women raised cougar kittens the same way in order to provide meat.

*****

While reading, Andrew paid no attention to Maria, only to be startled by the revelation that she was getting out of her jump suit.

Disrobing in front of him.

Offering herself to him.

She was in total shock.

Blocking out.

Oblivious to the fact that five great cougars would next turn their attention to Andrew and Maria once their savage work on the six point buck was finished.

The story of Joseph in Egypt flew through Andrew's brain.

Potipher's wife.

Throwing herself at Joseph.

Joseph fleeing the scene.

Leaving a piece of his clothing behind.

Potipher coming home.

His wife, the evil woman spurned, claiming she had been accosted by Joseph.

Potipher sending Joseph to prison.

Maria was moving toward him.

There was nowhere to run.

No way to escape.

Only like Daniel out with the lions.

In his mind, Andrew saw the Sheriff and her deputy, Betsy the owner of the diner, and the truckers including scantily clad tank top and cut offs long red mane truck driver, and his bishop, and his parents back in Salt Lake City, and Church ward members.

They were laughing at him and all the time the warm smell of Maria on the warm air from the heater enveloped him.

Not looking full at Maria, Andrew jerked the truck gear shift into gear.

Maria screamed.
Lurching forward, startling the five lions, two of which instantly jumped onto the hood, growling and swatting the windshield, eliciting repeated hysterical screams from Maria.

Maria holding her breath.

Still screaming.

Suffering from raw fear.

Hyperventilating.

"Do not hold your breath!" Andrew yelled.

Turning.

Backing up.

Turning again.

"Do not hold your breath!" Andrew shouted again and again.

Backing up.

Turning again.

Until truck, with dutiful trailer, carrying the two remaining black steeds, was turned around heading back toward Vernal the way they had come.

Not looking at Maria, Andrew stared straight ahead, driving, following the road as best he could, faster, then faster, until the truck was going twenty miles per hour.

Maria sobbing. Clutching at her jump suit. This comedic struggle to get back inside her jump suit and zip it up.
What possessed her Andrew could only guess.

"The trucker at the Vernal Diner may be right," thought Andrew. "Maybe she is no lady. Maybe Andrew I owe the red mane truck driver an apology. She's in terrible shock. Loss of Thomas. Loss of Jeb. Thomas poaching the buck. Traumatized by five mean starving cougars."

Maria was hysterical.

Her complexion was gray white like the gray white night snow.

This was her first close encounter with death.

Afraid of death.

Andrew's Joseph in Egypt flight response worked for time being.

It remained to be seen if Maria would think herself spurned and hold it against him or accuse him at later date.

Not knowing what to say, Andrew said, "You are a very attractive woman, Maria.

"You are way smart.

"I hold a Mormon temple recommend, Maria.

"I made a covenant with God to be chaste and marry a good woman in the Mormon temple for time and eternity."

Andrew stopped talking.

Nonplussed, Maria said nothing; and they inched their way on the winding snow covered one lane road gliding as it were through this moonlit ocean of snow.

Maria turned her face to the window.

Buried her head in her jacked.

She quietly sobbed.

*****

Not looking at him, with bowed head and hunched shoulders, she whispered. "I'm sorry, Andrew."

"That's all right," Andrew said. "Where is your family from?"

"Wetaskiwin, Alberta, Canada. By Edmonton," she said.

"How did you end up in Salt Lake City?" said Andrew.

"School. I applied for a math scholarship at the University of Utah and got it."

"Mathematics?" said Andrew.
"Yes. I have a Masters in Math?

"What's next?"

"Working on my doctorate."

"Then what?"

"Teach at a university or college."

Andrew was trying to draw Maria out, working to move her mind from tragedy, from danger they still were in, to thinking positive thoughts of survival.

Andrew turned on a country AM station out of San Diego.

AM radio signals propagate on the atmosphere at night and can travel from the U.S. to Canada, to Sweden or beyond.

Andrew drove onward while Maria crawled through the back of the truck into the camper.

She brought back a small handgun with bullets.
A Coleman lantern.

Binoculars.

Food.

Drink.

"There is a freezer full of meat. Multi-day survival packs. Sleeping bags. Blankets. A lantern. A twenty two rifle with shells." she whispered.

Andrew drove on - following the road toward Vernal hill after hill after hill as best he could.

Then, at top of a rise they were stuck.

Trapped in deep snow above the running boards.

Andrew missed the center of the road.

He gunned the truck.

Rocked it back and forth.

No avail.

With Thomas' night binoculars, Andrew could see five dark shapes following.

"Maria," Andrew said, so as not to trigger another round of screaming hysteria, "The cougars are not satisfied.

"They are not following us to lick deer blood from the roof.

"They have bigger prey in mind and we are it.

"If we stay here we freeze to death in the truck.

"If the cougars break into the truck we are cougar road kill.

"We need to take food, the two full gas cans, the snowmobiles, and run for it.

"So count to ten.

"Take a deep breath and run to the trailer door with me and back your snowmobile out and get ready to race for your life.

"I'll do the same.

"And give me the handgun and the twenty two rifle.

"I can't do it," she said.

"You have to do it," he said.

Andrew trudged in snow up to his thighs working his way round the truck to her door.

He opened it,

Andrew took hold of Maria's arm and jui jitsued her out of the truck, half carrying, half walking her back to the snowmobiles.

Andrew unloaded the two snowmobiles.

He cabled a can of gas to each snowmobile.

"Stay on the road just behind me," he said.

"Do not get out of my tracks.

"I repeat. Do not get out of my tracks!

"Do you hear me?
Maria nodded.

*****

Andrew took the meat from the freezer, steaks, bacon, eggs, sausage, syrup and spread them all over the truck, hoping diversion would buy time.

They mounted, started the snowmobiles, and gunned them down the narrow road into the night.

At top of a hill, Andrew looked back through night vision binoculars.

Five cougars were still following them.

"The cougars had stopped at the truck.

Andrew could see two of them on top of the camper.

Two were on the hood chewing the meat.

The big tom was not there which brought new fear to Andrew' mind.

The great tom cougar had not been persuaded to stop by a little bit of food.

In Iraq Andrew had used the AN-PVS-7.

It is one of the most recognized night vision combat proven devices in the world.
It was standard issue in Iraq.

It is a single tube, bi-ocular configuration that gives great night vision performance.

It comes with headgear, demist shields, sacrificial window, neck strap, and carrying case.

Thomas bought the expensive ATN Night Shadow 2, a night vision binocular with smart technology sensors that automatically turn on the night vision feature when the binocular is brought to viewing position.

Andrew scanned the landscape three hundred and sixty degrees.

There was smoke rising over a next set of low hills.

Maybe a ranch house.

Maybe a Bearskin Outfitter's camp, Andrew thought.

Andrew repeated in his mind what he had heard about Bearskin Outfitters.

That Peter and his men with the hunters more often than not camp at a hunt area and live in their heated camp trailers, spending no time in town and all the time hunting.

Driving the roads looking for cougar tracks.

When they find tracks they turn the hounds loose and the dogs chase and bay the cougar to a tree or rocky site.

Then the hunters walk in to shoot the eighty to one hundred and eighty pound cougar - the big toms weighing in at one hundred and thirty to one hundred and eighty pounds.

And all it takes is a cougar license which you get over the counter.

And you can add Bobcat or Elk or Mule Deer depending on which state you are in.

All for three thousand five hundred dollars to five thousand dollars to ten thousand dollars, to fifty thousand for a German or Japanese hunter who needs more amenities whatever those amenities might be.

For the time being, Andrew thought he would pass on Peter's offer to take him hunting.

Andrew didn't have a spare three thousand five hundred or five thousand dollars or ten thousand or fifty thousand.

When she saw the smoke, Maria took off in a straight line toward the smoke crossing what she thought was a field only to have Andrew in angry hot pursuit.

Andrew gunned his snowmobile past Maria to pull in front of her snowmobile and block her from continuing.

"Do you have a death wish," he yelled.

"Two or three more minutes and both of us will be frozen history somewhere at the bottom of this lake.

"You have got to stay on the road and follow me if we have any chance of survival."

Contrite, but sobbing, Maria turned her snowmobile to follow Andrew back to the road.

And all the time Andrew was praying they would not break through the ice.

*****

Over the next set of low hills Andrew could make out a set of dark buildings with smoke coming from the ranch house chimney.

Lights of Vernal were far off in the distance.

It was two in the morning.

The lights in the ranch house were out.

Through the curtains on the door, Andrew could outline the fireplace with its flickering fire.

Maria hid behind Andrew while Andrew knocked for the longest time to no answer.

He knocked louder and a sleepy rancher came to the door carrying a shotgun.

He was a young man.

Mid-thirties.

Hardened.

Tall.

Good looking.

Chiseled.

"Strong as a proverbial ox," thought Maria.

Intelligent.

Snow burned.

Worn by elements.

From riding horses.

Driving snowmobiles.

Working cattle.

Mowing, bailing, moving hay.

Brad was wary of strangers in black snowmobile garb knocking on his door at two am in the morning.

Andrew explained what had happened, apologizing for intruding this middle of the night intrusion.

Andrew told of the cougars tracking them.

Brad let Andrew and Maria inside and stoked the fire.

In pajamas and now wide awake, Brad's wife Jenny joined them.

The Petersons were not surprised by the thought of cougars following Andrew and Maria.

Brad stepped to the utility room next to the kitchen.

From what was a serious arsenal, Brad brought out three shotguns, two rifles and two handguns with ammunition.

Brad was no weak city man when it came to standing against danger.

If your home or your out buildings or animals or person were under siege, Brad was the fighting man you would want at your side.

Brad took charge.

He woke his two teenage daughters who were sleeping in a downstairs bedroom and sent them to the second floor with Jenny and Maria.

Brad gave a shotgun to Jenny and his oldest daughter.

Intuitively, Brad did not give Maria a gun.

Brad commanded, "You women barricade yourselves in the inside bedroom without windows.

"It is not likely one of those cougars will get through an upstairs window but we're not going to take the chance.

"Andrew and I will set watch on the stairs to protect you women and the home."

Brad stoked the fire in the fireplace and the two men waited.

"My dogs will tell us when the cougars come near the house and the barn."

*****

"My dad lived in this house with my grandparents," Brad told his story.

"Dad rode into Vernal one Saturday morning.

"He was twenty five years old.
"Stayed the day.

"Went to a church dance.

"Took my mother for an ice cream sundae.

"Right in the ice cream parlor, dad got down on one knee, showed her a diamond ring which he bought from a Sears Roebuck catalog, asked her to marry him, and was pleasantly surprised when she said yes.

"Dad went to meet her father to get his blessing.

"Her Dad said, will you provide for her and do you intend to marry her for time or time and eternity?

"Dad said 'time and eternity' and my Grandpa gave his blessing and dad and mom talked late into the evening making plans.

"They would get married in the Salt Lake Temple.

"They would have a reception in Salt Lake City for the family who traveled from out of town so they wouldn't have to drive to Vernal.

"They would have another reception in Vernal for local friends and neighbors.

"Anyway, it was late way after midnight when dad started for this house.

"Dad rode his favorite quarter horse stallion Jackson and it was cold beyond belief.

"Wind chill factor was fifty degrees off the charts.

"Dad was bundled up peeking through a peep hole.

"Not paying attention.

"Then he realized two big cougars were following him.

"Dad urged Jackson to a trot.

"Then a gallop.

"Then a dead run.

"Didn't do any good to push Jackson.

"Lions stayed right with him.

"Gaining on him.

"Dad was five hundred yards from the house and knew he couldn't make it.

"Cougars were close enough to attack and he just couldn't make the house.

"So what do you think my dad did?"

"Don't know," said Andrew. "Must have made it to the house since you are here?"

Brad continued his story, "Dad slowed Jackson to a walk, pulled out his revolver and right there in the middle of the road shot Jackson dead.

"Dad stepped out of his saddle, took off his cowboy boots, and ran.

"The cougars stopped to eat the horse and dad made it to the house.
"But the story doesn't end there.

"What do you think dad did next?"

"Don't know," said Andrew.

"Dad was so flaming angry at those two cougars that he took his over under rifle shotgun, loaded his pockets with shells, walked straight back to the dead horse and now gorged cougars.

"He walked right up to them and shot the two of them dead.

"Skinned them on the spot.

"Brought the heads and skins back to the house and hung them in one of the sheds.

"Cured the hides and the heads and those two cougars were throw rugs in the living room 'til the day Dad died.

"Dad never got tired of telling his cougar story and I don't either."

By this time the dogs were barking out of control.

*****

Even though the dogs were locked inside one of the sheds, they knew the lions had entered the yard and they were scared to death.

With moonlight on the snow it was easy for Andrew to watch the five cougars from the window.

They knew we were in the house.

They circled the house, then the barn, then the sheds, looking for a way in.

But Brad had been thorough.

There was no point of entry.

Three of them circled the house.

Through the windows, the two men watched three cougars climb a tree next to the house.

They heard them leap onto the roof.

They could hear the big cats walking on the roof.
Brad said, "You can bet they will find the fireplace chimney."

Sure enough.

Brad hadn't gotten those words out of his mouth before one cougar, then two, then three came down the chimney in a cloud of soot and smoke.

Two shotguns roared killing two of the cougars.

The third was lightly wounded.

As the third cougar sprang Brad and Andrew simultaneously pumped and fired.

They had two dead cougars on the floor in the living room and a third cougar dead at the foot of the stairs.

"Still two to go," said Brad. "Two of them didn't climb the tree."

"The great tom and one other," said Andrew.

"There is only one other way into the house," said Brad.

"Through the windows," said Andrew.

The men reloaded.

They stood half way up the stairs facing the downstairs windows.

Waiting was excruciating.

A large grandfather clock ticked.

It chimed.

It ticked off more time.

It chimed.

It was four thirty am.

In massive rage, the great tom cougar exploded through a side window of the house, showering glass everywhere.

Another huge cougar followed close behind.

The two men fired the shotguns, stunning the big cats.

They found the rifles, shot, and five great cougars lay dead.

Working together, they dragged the cats outside the house onto the porch, covered up the broken window, started a fire in the fireplace, and cleaned up the cougar blood.

*****

Brad, Lisa and the girls went to bed.

Maria slept in the center bedroom the women had barricaded.

Andrew slept on the couch in the living room.

Before going to sleep Brad called 911 to explain what had just happened.

Sometime after lunch the Sheriff and his two deputies got to the ranch house where they conducted separate interrogation of Andrew, Maria and the Petersons.

The Sheriff threatened a polygraph but backed down after he got a good look at the cougars and after Maria and Jenny in separate interviews corroborated what Andrew and Brad told them.

The sheriff notified the family of Thomas and Jeb, organized a search party, and Andrew led them back to a place on the road where he could see the tree with the cross bar.

Divers found the bodies after several hours diving.

*****

Back in Salt Lake City, Andrew was more than exhausted.

Home but not in time to teach his Sunday school class about Joseph's escape from Potipher's wife.

The next Thursday was a double viewing plus combined funeral for Thomas and Jeb.

Andrew spoke at the funeral.

Maria was in the audience.

Andrew spoke of –

the ocean of life undulating like snow far beyond our visual horizons –

terrible laws of nature –

staying on the road –

snow and life preparation and survival –

being a marine laying it all on the line to protect country and cause –

the shortness of mortality --

 the quickness of death –

the tree and its cross bar –

the huge tom cougar tempting man to his death –

black snowmobiles and helmet symbols of darkness –

 Magnum and Savage guns as instruments of violence and death –

 Christ's Gethsemane, crucifixion and resurrection –

 terrible nature of jealousy, enmity, and hatred –

 love and forgiveness despite how others might feel about you –

 prayer during crisis --

of being prepared when attacked by five great cougars.

Footnote 1: Sources and Notes

Bear Paw Outfitters Web Site

By My Rifle, the creed of a United States Marine, by Major General WH Rupertus, Internet

Cougar Safety Tips, Kodiak Wildlife Products Inc. Web Site

Cougars, Internet

Cougars, Cheyenne Legend, Internet

Ford F-150 Truck, Internet

History of Vernal, Doris K. Burton, Utah History Encyclopedia, Internet

Magnum and Savage Guns, Internet

Nimrod, Internet

Plott Hounds, Internet

Redbone Coonhounds, Internet

The Book Cliffs, BLM Web Site

Welcome to Vernal Web Site

Yamaha Snowmobiles, Internet

Footnote 2: Marriage for Time and Eternity

"The Church of Jesus Christ of Latter-day Saints (Mormon) believe marriage under the law of the gospel and the holy priesthood is for eternity, and that men and women thus sealed in marriage continue to have children throughout eternity. Although this concept of marriage is not fully presented in our present Bible, traces of it are found in Matthew 16:16-19; 19:3-8; 22:23-30; Pearl of Great Price, Moses 4:18; Doctrine & Covenants 132." See www.lds.org and www.mormon.org

Footnote 3: One of the best short summaries of LDS Church belief

THE ARTICLES OF FAITH
OF THE CHURCH OF JESUS CHRIST OF LATTER-DAY SAINTS

History of the Church, Vol. 4, pp. 535—541

1 WE believe in God, the Eternal Father, and in His Son, Jesus Christ, and in the Holy Ghost.

2 We believe that men will be punished for their own sins, and not for Adam's transgression.

3 We believe that through the Atonement of Christ, all mankind may be saved, by obedience to the laws and ordinances of the Gospel.

4 We believe that the first principles and ordinances of the Gospel are: first, Faith in the Lord Jesus Christ; second, Repentance; third, Baptism by immersion for the remission of sins; fourth, Laying on of hands for the gift of the Holy Ghost.

5 We believe that a man must be called of God, by prophecy, and by the laying on of hands by those who are in authority, to preach the Gospel and administer in the ordinances thereof.

6 We believe in the same organization that existed in the Primitive Church, namely, apostles, prophets, pastors, teachers, evangelists, and so forth.

7 We believe in the gift of tongues, prophecy, revelation, visions, healing, interpretation of tongues, and so forth.

8 We believe the Bible to be the word of God as far as it is translated correctly; we also believe the Book of Mormon to be the word of God.

9 We believe all that God has revealed, all that He does now reveal, and we believe that He will yet reveal many great and important things pertaining to the Kingdom of God.

10 We believe in the literal gathering of Israel and in the restoration of the Ten Tribes; that Zion (the New Jerusalem) will be built upon the American continent; that Christ will reign personally upon the earth; and, that the earth will be renewed and receive its paradisiacal glory.

11 We claim the privilege of worshiping Almighty God according to the dictates of our own conscience, and allow all men the same privilege, let them worship how, where, or what they may.

12 We believe in being subject to kings, presidents, rulers, and magistrates, in obeying, honoring, and sustaining the law.

13 We believe in being honest, true, chaste, benevolent, virtuous, and in doing good to all men; indeed, we may say that we follow the admonition of Paul—We believe all things, we hope all things, we have endured many things, and hope to be able to endure all things. If there is anything virtuous, lovely, or of good report or praiseworthy, we seek after these things.

JOSEPH SMITH

Footnote 4: Cougar Safety

Outdoor Wisdom
- Never go near a cougar.
- Keep children close when hiking.
- Hike in small groups.
- Take a heavy walking stick and weapon.

If you see sign of a cougar or see a cougar
- Stop.
- Don't run.
- Pick up and shelter small children.
- Spread your arms or coat to look as large as possible.
- Keep eye contact with a cougar.
- Try to back up slowly and escape.

If threatened or attacked
- Attack.
- Assert yourself.
- Shout.
- Wave your arms.
- Throw rocks or sticks.

Footnote 5: An Allegory

An allegory is a parable representative and symbolic of and implying spiritual meanings and truths by means of material, concrete physical forms and actual or fictional stories of real life.

199 Ways To Make Your Good Marriage Great or Your Bad Marriage Better

Romance and improve your marriage today

RICHARD W. LINFORD

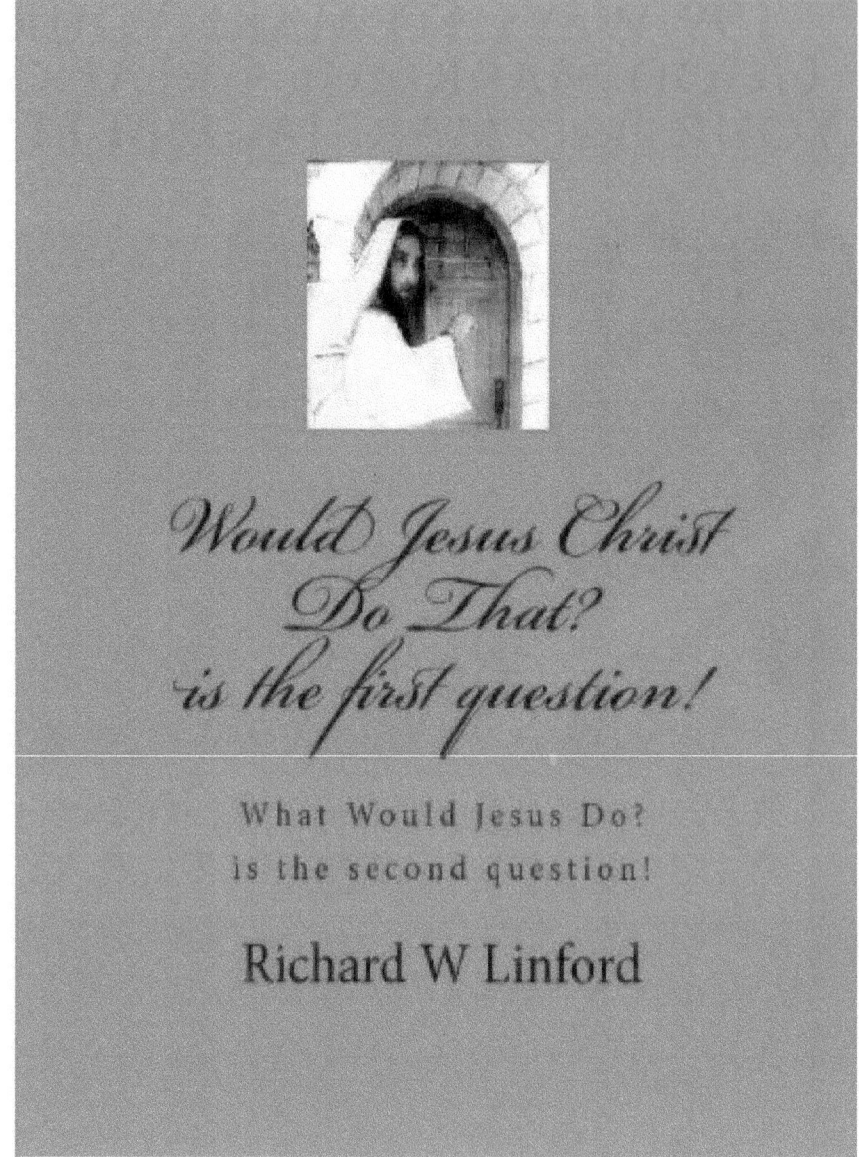

Andrew Chipman's Christmas Angel

Richard W. Linford

Books by the author

Would Jesus Christ Do That? is the first question! What Would Jesus Do? is the second question!

Andrew Chipman's Christmas Angel

199 Ways to Make Your Good Marriage Great or Your Bad Marriage Better

The Young Marine and the Snow

Order at www.amazon.com. http://www.amazon.com/s/ref=nb_ss_b?url=search-alias%3Dstripbooks&field-keywords=Richard+W.+Linford

Author's note

I work at being a good husband, father, grandpa, and neighbor. I am a Christian and active member of The Church of Jesus Christ of Latter-day Saints (Mormon). I served in the Church as a lay bishop and a member of several stake presidencies. I am a businessman, attorney at law, writer, artist, and sometime golfer and was state chairman of The National Conference of Christians of Jews and on the NCCJ national board for many years. I was chairman of the multi-county Red Cross and served on the American Heart Association and Junior Achievement Boards.

We are children of God our Heavenly Father. I dedicate this small work to The United States Marines and to my family and to you regardless of your religion or belief system.

"Be not afraid" and "be of good cheer" are words of Jesus Christ I find especially comforting. I pray you may have great health, happiness, and exceptional prosperity!

Richard Linford

My Blog is http://jesus-isthechrist.blogspot.com/

Websites about my faith you may find interesting are www.lds.org and www.mormon.org.

The Young Marine and the Snow

an allegory

Richard W. Linford

www.ingramcontent.com/pod-product-compliance
Lightning Source LLC
Chambersburg PA
CBHW080524110426
42742CB00017B/3225